Original title:
Tales from the Thicket

Copyright © 2025 Creative Arts Management OÜ
All rights reserved.

Author: Juliette Kensington
ISBN HARDBACK: 978-1-80567-178-7
ISBN PAPERBACK: 978-1-80567-477-1

Where the Wild Ones Roam

In the meadow where critters play,
A sloth tried to race, but slept all day.
A squirrel wore shades, struck a cool pose,
While a turtle debated how fast he goes.

A rabbit cracked jokes, oh quite the tease,
While a hedgehog rolled by, awakening the bees.
With laughter that echoed, they danced and spun,
In a party of fur, it was all just fun.

Tales of the Whispering Bush

In the thicket, where whispers grow,
A fox wore a hat, putting on a show.
The frogs wore bow ties, croaked in delight,
While fireflies twinkled, lighting the night.

The owls cracked puns, with wisdom so sly,
While the raccoons begged, 'Just one more pie!'
Laughter erupted, in the cool evening air,
A circus of creatures, without a care.

The Veil of the Nightingale

Under moonlight, a nightingale sings,
While a crow juggles bones, oh, the joy that brings.
With whispers of giggles, the shadows play,
As the raccoon tries dancing, in a clumsy way.

A mockingbird mimicked, the laughter so bright,
As a shy little mouse joined the festive night.
With critters united, so cozy and near,
They turned the dark veil into one filled with cheer.

Chronicles of the Sunlit Clearing

In the sunlit grove, where the daisies bloom,
A bear in a tutu danced by the room.
The mice held a tea, with tiny fine cups,
While a peacock spread tales, then tripped on his up.

A badger recited, poetry in rhyme,
While the bunnies played hopscotch, wasting no time.
With the warmth of the sun, they all felt so free,
Creating sweet memories, eternally glee.

Harmonies of the Serpent's Coils

In the grass, the snakes all dance,
With wiggly moves that leave us in a trance.
They sing to bugs in silly rhymes,
While plotting pranks and silly crimes.

A viper tried to charm a bird,
But ended up just looking absurd.
With a tangled tail and a wink of glass,
He slipped right by, but missed the grass.

Whispers of the Wilderness

Squirrels chatter like gossip queens,
Discussing the latest nuts and beans.
With bushy tails and sneaky views,
They laugh at the deer in their brand new shoes.

The owls hoot in rhythmic jest,
While planning who they'll scare the best.
A feathered friend with a crooked beak,
Winks at the rabbits, who peek and squeak.

Secrets Beneath the Canopy

Beneath the leaves, where shadows play,
The critters plot their crafty way.
A beetle tries to steal a clover,
While a lazy toad just rolls over.

A wise old fox with a glinting eye,
Invents new games to pass the time by.
He hides in logs, plays peek-a-boo,
As dreams of mischief spiral anew.

The Heartbeat of the Woods

In the woods, the laughter swells,
As creatures share their secret spells.
A rabbit hops on a bouncy tune,
While a raccoon sings to the brightening moon.

The trees nod along with a gentle sway,
Tickling the leaves in a cheeky play.
With whispers and giggles that rise and fall,
Nature's humor is the best of all.

The Lure of Twisting Vines

In a thicket thick where the critters play,
A squirrel once found a vine to sway.
He twirled and he whirled in a dizzy race,
Until he got stuck, oh what a face!

The rabbits all laughed, they couldn't believe,
As the squirrel yelled out, 'Where's my reprieve?'
With a tug and a pull, they freed their friend,
Now he guards that vine, his pride to defend.

Songs of the Hidden Grove

In the hidden grove where shadows dance,
A frog took a leap, he fancied romance.
With a ribbit and croak, he sang so loud,
The trees shook their leaves; he thrilled the crowd.

But the song took a turn, as frogs do know,
He tripped on a root and fell below.
The owls hooted softly, what a sight to see,
A croaky serenade gone topsy-turvy.

Legends from the Leafy Realm

Once in a realm where the foliage sprawled,
A raccoon named Ralph played tricks, enthralled.
He stole from the picnic with stealth and with flair,
But slipped on a pie, oh how he did flare!

The ants held a meeting with crumbs as their prize,
Discussing the mischief with wide, tiny eyes.
Ralph vowed to be careful, yet chuckled with glee,
For who didn't love a good slice—especially a spree?

Murmurs of the Shaded Path

Along the shaded path, the whispers alive,
A tortoise named Tim had a sprint to deprive.
He said to the hare, 'Just wait and you'll see,
I can run with the best, just you watch me!'

But as Tim plodded on, slow as a breeze,
He spotted a snack—oh, what a tease!
He nibbled and munched, time slipped right away,
While the hare snoozed on, 'Til the end of the day.

Whispers in the Underbrush

In the thicket, critters scheme,
Squirrels plotting quite the dream.
With acorns piled in a tower,
They giggle at the midnight hour.

Rabbits dance with silly hops,
While owls talk and never stop.
A hedgehog wears a tiny hat,
And shouts, 'I'm the king of that!'

Each rustle tells a cheeky joke,
From the owl to the badger folk.
The laughter bounces off the trees,
As flowers sway with gentle tease.

The forest hums with playful mirth,
A bug parade for all it's worth.
With whispers carried by the breeze,
They share their tales and giggle with ease.

Secrets of the Verdant Grove

The trees conspire, leaves a-twitch,
'A frog sings opera!' says a rich.
The hedgehog dreams of dancing bears,
While fireflies play tag in pairs.

Wily fox stretches with a yawn,
Plotting mischief at the dawn.
A parrot paints the night's first twirl,
While the whole grove spins and swirls.

With acorns tossed in silly games,
Each critter teases the others' names.
The brook joins in with gurgling glee,
As laughter echoes through the trees.

Secrets shared with morning's light,
Squirrel grants the wise owl flight.
All is jolly in this patch,
In verdant groves where dreams can hatch.

Shadows Beneath the Canopy

Underneath the leafy roofs,
Moles gossip in adorable goofs.
A shy deer with a twitchy ear,
Laughs at a chipmunk's tale of fear.

Crickets sing with playful sound,
While shadows dance upon the ground.
A raccoon wears a crown of rue,
And swears to join the royal crew.

The musty air is filled with cheer,
As everyone draws close to hear.
A badger jokes about the night,
In whispers soft, they share delight.

So when the moon begins to rise,
And twinkling stars adorn the skies,
The shadows play their merry role,
In this enchanted woodland stroll.

Echoes of the Hidden Hollow

In the hollow where echoes play,
A tortoise speaks in riddles gay.
With every shell and every laugh,
The creatures take a silly path.

A ruckus stirs the quiet night,
As critters gather for a bite.
The mouse comically slides on leaf,
Claiming he's the king of beef.

The lanterns glow with tiny smiles,
As everyone shares their loony styles.
A wise old turtle hums a tune,
Beneath the watchful, winking moon.

With laughter echoing through the trees,
In hidden hollows, all are pleased.
The fun continues, hearts so light,
As woodland friends embrace the night.

Secrets of the Sweet Scented Earth

In a garden of wonder, where daisies play,
The worms tell a joke that makes flowers sway.
Bees wear tiny hats, sipping nectar with flair,
While the carrots dance, thinking life isn't rare.

The onions are laughing, they bubble with glee,
Tickling the turnips, oh, what a spree!
Frogs on the lilies, doing their jig,
While hedgehogs join in, all sing, "We're so big!"

Underneath the soil, the moles have a show,
Hosting a party for critters below.
With fungi as lights, and roots digging deep,
The secrets are shared, as they giggle and leap.

In this fragrant realm, where laughter grows strong,
The earth's little secrets, they whistle a song.

The Meadow's Secret Song

In a meadow so bright, where the daisies conspire,
Grasshoppers chirp as they dance on the wire.
The butterflies chuckle with the bumblebees,
And the daisies are gossiping with the trees.

A rabbit with spectacles reads out a tale,
While squirrels are prancing, their laughter won't fail.
The sunflowers nod, sharing dreams of the sky,
And the breeze joins in, with a jaunty "Oh my!"

A picnic of ants, crumbs strewn to the side,
As the caterpillar plays, oh, what a ride!
The thistles are gossiping, sharing their fears,
Amidst all the chuckles, they wipe happy tears.

In this meadow of mirth, joy is the tune,
As every little creature dances beneath the moon.

Legends of the Winding Stream

By the giggling brook, the fish tell a joke,
As turtles float by, with a wink they provoke.
The rocks have a giggle, the current's a laugh,
While the frogs join the fun on the log's sunny path.

A heron in sneakers struts with such pride,
As minnows make ripples, their laughter won't hide.
The dragonflies buzz, buzzing tales so absurd,
While the otters are tumbling, tails twirled and blurred.

In the splash of the water, the echoes resound,
With quacking and splashing, pure joy can be found.
Each ripple has secrets, each wave has a rhyme,
As the stream shares its legends, one splash at a time.

In this playful domain, where mischief runs free,
The laughter cascades, like the leaves on the tree.

Whispers from the Woodland Shadows

In the shadows where whispers tickle the night,
Raccoons are plotting what treats they'll invite.
The owls spin their yarns, in a twist of delight,
As the moon shines down, casting silvery light.

A fox with a flair, wearing spectacles grand,
Shares stories of mischief, dark tea in his hand.
The rabbits all giggle, with carrots they toast,
To the tales of the thicket, they love the most.

The mushrooms are nodding, their caps tipped with glee,
As the shadows tell secrets that none can foresee.
The night critters chuckle, a woodland brigade,
With laughter echoing, in a moonbeam parade.

In this woodland of whimsy, where fun seems to dwell,
Every creature can sing, and all laughter swells.

Beneath the Boughs' Embrace

A squirrel danced in a silly hat,
He claimed to be the king of that.
With acorns tucked beneath each arm,
He charmed the birds with silly charm.

A rabbit laughed at the funny sight,
Said, "Your majesty, you're quite a fright!"
The trees all shook with muffled glee,
As the king squirrel waved his paw so free.

A turtle came in a bright green sock,
And joined the squirrel's wobbly mock.
Together they wobbled, they jumped and spun,
Making laughter spread like rays of sun.

Beneath the boughs, where the shadows play,
All critters gather at the end of day.
With giggles and jokes, they spin a tale,
In the great green forest, where silliness prevails.

Moments in the Moonlit Thicket

The moonlight danced on a snoozy owl,
He snorted awake, sounding just like a growl.
"Who's there?" he hooted, in voice so deep,
But soon dozed off, drifting into sleep.

By the brook, a frog croaked a tune,
His voice echoed bright under the moon.
With each croak, he did a little jig,
A splashy performance, truly big!

The fireflies flickered, like stars on land,
Winking at critters, who all took a stand.
They formed a conga in a merry parade,
With laughter and music, their worries wereayed.

In moments like this, with friends all around,
The moonlit thicket held joy profound.
With silly antics, and fun on display,
Every night brought new games to play.

The Storyteller's Refuge in the Brush

In the brush where stories swirl and twine,
A hedgehog recited a tale divine.
With each little prick, he'd add a point,
His audience laughed, they'd never disappoint.

A fox in a vest tried to take a turn,
But forgot his lines; the crowd did yearn.
"I once saw a cat that danced on a fence!"
He stumbled and tripped, which made good sense.

The raccoons howled with laughter so loud,
As the fox turned bright red, so very cowed.
Yet with every blunder, the fun only grew,
For in the wild brush, these tales felt true.

A party of critters, each one unique,
Found joy in the silliness, week after week.
In the storyteller's refuge, with giggles and hush,
Life's greatest adventures hid deep in the brush.

Whispers from the Thicket's Edge

In a thicket where critters play,
A squirrel dropped acorns all day.
It thought it could hoard them just fine,
But tripped on a vine, oh the design!

Sneaky rabbits plotting a feast,
With lettuce so green, they had to at least,
Nibble some carrots, but what a shock,
The gardener watched, they ran like a clock!

A raccoon with a mask, quite the crew,
Stole snacks from a picnic, that much is true.
But slipped on a banana, a slip and a slide,
Now he rules the park with comedic pride!

The Enchanted Pathway of Shadows

Down an enchanted pathway, so bright,
A gnome tried to dance, what a sight!
With shoes too large and a hat to match,
He twirled and he whirled, then fell with a scratch!

The shadows giggled, they saw the fall,
While fireflies flickered, lighting up all.
A grumpy old frog croaked a loud cheer,
"That's dance in my book! Come join my beer!"

Tipsy owls hooted, lost in their fun,
They thought it was night, but it was noon sun!
With winks and wise cracks, they'd share their tales,
Of one-legged pigeons and flirting snails!

Carved in Canopies

In the canopies, where the birds sing,
A woodpecker carved out a comedic fling.
He knocked on a tree, it echoed all round,
But startled a bee, now that bee's quite wound!

A wise old owl with glasses too thick,
Said, "Watch out my friend, or you'll face a quick kick!"
The woodpecker laughed, and he knocked once more,
And the bee buzzed back, "You just upped the score!"

Leaves whispered secrets, a riddle or two,
Trees chuckled loudly, as if they all knew.
And the woodpecker danced, as butterflies swayed,
In trees filled with laughter, where no joke had stayed!

Myths of the Murmuring Stream

By the murmuring stream, legends abound,
Where fish tell tales of the lost and found.
A catfish in glasses swears he can see,
The secrets of minnows who swim wild and free!

A turtle turned wizard, or so he proclaimed,
With spells made of pond water, easily tamed.
He turned a leaf into a hopping frog,
Who croaked out a joke while stuck in the bog!

The ducks formed a choir, quacking their tune,
Complaining of shadows, a pas de deux moon.
With ripples of laughter, and splashes of cheer,
The stream weaves its myths, never a dull year!

Murmured Memories of the Meadow

In the meadow, bees do prance,
Chasing flowers, never a chance.
A cow moos softly, says hello,
While rabbits hop around, on the go.

Squirrels chatter, plotting their heist,
Stealing acorns, oh how they're biased!
A snail moves slowly, joins the spree,
Laughing at the rush, 'Come dance with me!'

The sun shines bright, the grass is green,
A duck quacks loud, likes to be seen.
A hedgehog grumbles, finding a hole,
Surprised by a worm who stole its role.

Laughter echoes, a joyful crowd,
Each critter's tales, both funny and loud.
In this place, where silliness thrives,
Every day feels like joyful lives.

Shadows Dancing with the Stars

At dusk the shadows learn to jive,
Fireflies join in, buzzing alive.
A raccoon wearing a tiny hat,
Sways to the rhythm, oh fancy that!

The owl hoots softly, keeping the beat,
While crickets chirp in time to the heat.
A field mouse waltzes, proud on the grass,
Caught in a twirl, hopes the night lasts.

Under the moon, where secrets gleam,
Frogs leap high, living their dream.
A misplaced acorn starts up the jam,
The hedgehogs giggle, 'Oh yes, who's the ham?'

In this party where whimsy reigns,
Silly dances wash away the pains.
As laughter mingles with the stars,
Even the night finds a few avatars.

The Hidden Chorus of the Canopy

Up in the trees, a chorus sings,
Parrots squawk and add their flings.
A squirrel on branch, too proud of its show,
Accidentally drops an acorn below.

The raccoons clap, they love the tune,
While shadows play under the moon.
A toad joins in with a croaky cheer,
Echoing laughter, ring loud and clear.

With the breeze, leaves sway and swing,
Perfumed whispers of nature's bling.
A wise old owl surveys the scene,
Chortling softly, 'A sight so keen!'

The canopy whispers secrets shy,
Of all the antics beneath the sky.
With winged mischief, laughter ignites,
And nocturnal dreams continue their flights.

Serendipitous Stories of the Thickets

In thickets and groves, treasure lies,
A wiggle here, a fluttered surprise.
A badger's giggle, a rabbit's wink,
All tangled up by the corner's brink.

A porcupine prances, feeling so bold,
Wearing a crown made of marigold.
Every critter shares a funny lore,
With wild imaginations that shake the floor.

An opossum playing dead for laughs,
Mistaking a twig for cobweb's chaffs.
The fox rolls over, can't take the tease,
While birds drop in to spread some ease.

In this jungle of chatter and cheer,
Each creature whispers, 'Oh come near!'
Unraveling tales both goofy and bright,
Where every mischief shines in the night.

Ballads of the Brave Little Creatures

In the grass, they dance with cheer,
A mouse with a crown, oh dear!
Singing songs, oh, quite absurd,
A fly leads them, how they've stirred!

The frogs leap high, but land on fate,
A toad hops by, it's just too late.
With tiny drums, they make a sound,
A performance, no one's around!

"A snail's the best, a champion," says
The crickets who jump in wild arrays.
A ladybug spins like a top,
And everyone laughs till they drop!

With acorns tossed like frozen pies,
Squirrels giggle, oh how they fly!
Against a tree, they play and squeal,
Life's simple joys, so very real.

Secrets of the Evergreen Enclave

Under boughs where whispers teem,
A raccoon plots his midnight scheme.
With sticky paws, he swipes a snack,
But that cat's there; oh, what a flack!

The owls hoot, "What's night without fun?"
They dabble in games till the sun.
A dance-off starts, feathers and fur,
With each crazy move, they all confer!

A hedgehog wears a tiny hat,
He spins around, thought he was flat!
The secret's out, a party's to be,
In the woods, with giggles, wild and free.

"Don't eat my stash!" the acorn shouts,
As squirrels tease, leaping about.
They poke their noses, curious and spry,
While laughter echoes under the sky.

Anecdotes from the Twilight Thorns

In twilight's glow, a bug sits bright,
Telling tales of a daring flight.
Past thorny bushes, oh what a chase,
With briars laughing, keeping pace!

The fireflies flicker, starlight's kin,
While the beetles join in, grinning within.
A snail proclaims, "I've outrun you!"
But honestly, it's the slowest crew.

With dinner served on a petal plate,
They feast till dawn, oh, isn't it great?
A thief in shadow, a thieving bat,
He drops a grape, how dull is that!

The moonbeam shines, whispers weave,
While creatures laugh, no time to grieve.
In thorny thickets, joy won't cease,
For every tale brings giggles, sweet peace.

Emblems of the Nature's Heart

Three rabbits play poker, what a sight!
Their wily ways bring giggles bright.
With acorn chips, they ponder their fate,
While the fox, just watches—oh, isn't it great?

A weasel whispers, "Take his bluff!"
The shadows flicker, these critters tough.
With stalking grace, they plot and scheme,
For nature's heart holds the funniest dream!

A turtle's slow, but he's got the look,
Reads the rules from a duck with a book.
With wing and shell, they break all norms,
Creating chaos in silly forms.

"Next round's my turn," the skunk will snark,
While everyone tenses, hoping for dark.
In nature's embrace, laughter can start,
These brave little souls own nature's heart.

The Mystery of Mossy Stones

In the forest, rocks are sly,
They sneak around, oh my, oh my!
Covered in green, they play pretend,
Come to life, their mischief won't end.

Bouncing about in a goofy dance,
Rolling stones just seek romance!
A ladybug joins in the fun,
While ants march by, all on the run.

Swapping tales of their wild night,
Mossy stones glimmer in moonlight.
Crickets chirp a lullaby song,
As the forest laughs right along.

So if you stroll where shadows collide,
Beware of laughs that won't be denied!
For mossy stones with eyes so bright,
Will tickle your toes with pure delight.

Enchanted Breezes of the Foliage

Whispers float on breezes dear,
Leaves giggle as they start to steer.
Branches sway like they know a joke,
Tickling noses, they laugh and poke.

A feathered friend joins the spree,
Singing tunes of glee and glee.
The sun beams down, all gleeful too,
Painting smiles in the morning dew.

When gusts arrive with a playful shove,
Make leaves paparazzi, oh how they love!
Chasing shadows, they twirl about,
Becoming a whirl of silliness, no doubt.

So follow the winds, take a chance,
Join foliage in their goofy dance.
For in the breeze, laughter's the key,
Unlocking giggles, wild and free.

Dance of the Flickering Fireflies

In the meadow, lights do sway,
Flickering fireflies in a display.
They spin and twirl in a shining race,
A glowworm's party, what a wild place!

With lazy hops and jolly grins,
These tiny dancers let the fun begin.
Chasing shadows, they play peek-a-boo,
Twinkling bright, in skies so blue.

A bug in a bow tie takes to the stage,
Waving to flowers as if they were sage.
The moon chuckles, enjoying the show,
As night creatures gather, putting on a glow.

So join this jig, let yourself be light,
In the glow of the stars, all feels just right.
For fireflies dance with secrets untold,
Bringing laughter, as the night unfolds.

The Burrows' Secret Tales

In burrows deep, the critters meet,
Sharing snacks and giggling sweet.
Squirrels spin yarns, while rabbits munch,
A feast unfolds, a funny brunch.

Badgers tell tales of slimy mud,
While otters slide with a joyful thud.
A hedgehog sings quite out of key,
But everyone laughs, they're wild and free!

Raccoons trade stories of shiny things,
While moles wiggle, showing off their bling.
In the cozy burrows, joy prevails,
As laughter echoes through secret trails.

So if you hear whispers from below,
Know burrows are bustling with giggles and glow.
Join the crew, be part of the fun,
In this world where laughter is never done.

The Labyrinth of Green Dreams

In a maze of leaves, we play hide and seek,
The bushes giggle, the trees start to peek.
A squirrel on a branch quips a joke from above,
While rabbits engage in a dance of pure love.

The hedgehogs roll by, all dressed in their spines,
They boast of their travels, sipping berry wines.
The sun filters in, making shadows parade,
We laugh till we're dizzy, in this leafy charade.

A tapestry woven with laughter and cheer,
Each twist of the path whispers secrets we hear.
The moon may be watching, but she's just as bemused,
In the labyrinth green, we are happily confused.

Lurking Spirits of the Wilderness

In the thicket they loom, with playful delight,
Ghosts with a giggle, in the pale moonlight.
They tickle the ferns and ruffle the grass,
Chasing away shadows as the night hours pass.

A raccoon in a top hat, what a sight to behold,
With a twirl of his cane, oh, he's daring and bold.
The owls hoot in laughter, sharing a jest,
As the spirits concoct their wild nightly quest.

They swing from the branches, they sway with the breeze,
A whimsical rendezvous, aiming to please.
In this wild frolic, where fun has no bounds,
The lurking spirits dance, to nature's sweet sounds.

Requiem for Rustling Leaves

Oh leaves, so merry, with secrets to share,
With whispers and giggles as they twirl in the air.
They conjure up stories of pranks and of play,
As autumn's last dance bids the summer goodbye day.

A chipmunk darts past, calling out, "What's your loot?"
While a squirrel joins in, "I've pilfered your fruit!"
The leaves rustle louder, filled with tiny glee,
Their requiem is a laugh, a wild jubilee.

As the wind carries tales, through branches they fly,
Beneath the bright sky, we watch nature sigh.
Yet in this farewell, there's still so much cheer,
For in every soft crunch, new stories appear.

The Whispered Promise of the Woods

Amidst the tall pines, where mischief does bloom,
The whispers of promise hang low with perfume.
A bear with a grin shares the sweetest of snacks,
    While a fox tosses riddles into our tracks.

Squirrels hold court with their curious schemes,
Crafting wild plans beneath sunbeams and dreams.
The woods full of chatter, what secrets they keep,
With sounds of the branches that giggle and leap.

In this merry realm, where the playful abound,
Each whisper a memory in nature's grand sound.
With laughter as currency, the days drift away,
    The promise of woods is forever in play.

Fables of the Eldritch Thorns

In shadows where the hedgehogs dance,
A cactus tried to woo a prance.
It forgot its spines, oh what a sight,
The rabbits laughed and took to flight.

A wily fox in boots of gold,
Seduced a snail with tales of old.
But when he tripped, his glitter flew,
The party turned to hide and boo!

A tortoise spun a yarn so tall,
About the time he ran a mall.
Yet every deal, it seemed to hail,
Was just a leaf, a twig, a tail!

The chattering squirrels took a vote,
To crown a crow who wore a coat.
But when he flew to fetch a snack,
He turned around and found no back!

Portraits of the Gnarled Roots

The roots began to gossip, quick,
About a tree that danced a trick.
It asked for rain, but got a shoe,
And all the trees just laughed and grew.

A sprout claimed it could sing at night,
But croaked a tune that gave a fright.
Still, owls hooted tunes of cheer,
While crickets held their ears in fear.

A wise old oak, with splinters neat,
Challenged a vine to a dance feat.
But every twirl, the vine would bend,
And tangled up its leafy friend!

The roots held contests of who could grow,
But with every twist, they brought a show.
And when the sun began to set,
All laughed at how they never met!

Fantasies of the Moonlit Clearing

In moonlit fields where shadows crew,
A rabbit sneezed, and off he flew.
The dance of fireflies lit the way,
As mushrooms whispered secrets gray.

An owl in spectacles read aloud,
To a crowd of critters, quite a crowd.
But as he spoke of laws and rules,
A raccoon shouted, "You're all fools!"

A hedgehog juggled acorns bold,
While mockingbirds sang tales retold.
The laughter echoed through the night,
As every creature joined the fright!

With nightingale tunes soaring high,
They laughed until the stars could cry.
And when dawn broke, they all took flight,
The clearing giggled, "What a night!"

Parables of the Breezy Boughs

High above where breezes play,
The winds conspired, day by day.
A squirrel tried to kite the breeze,
But ended up with just bare knees.

A chubby robin claimed to soar,
But forgot how to close the door.
It flapped and landed with a thud,
In a bush of blue and cheerful bud!

Those breezy boughs held tales of pranks,
With whispers swirling, filled with thanks.
And on a branch, a crow would croon,
About a frog who aimed for noon!

Yet as they all began to jest,
The winds came blowing, putting to test.
With laughter loud, they took a dive,
And found their joy was still alive!

Echoes of the Twilit Haven

In the woods where shadows play,
A rabbit pranced in a fray.
With a wiggle and a hop,
He made the fireflies stop.

A squirrel in a tiny hat,
Sipped tea like an urban brat.
He spilled it on a log so wide,
And laughed as it slipped and slid.

The crickets joined a merry tune,
As the raccoon danced 'neath the moon.
With a wink and a cheeky grin,
He twirled like he'd outsmarted kin.

Laughter echoed through the air,
Unexpected joys are everywhere.
In a thicket full of glee,
Nature's jesters dance wild and free.

The Puzzle of Twisted Roots

Beneath a tree with twisted roots,
A fox in a cloak tried on some boots.
He tripped and tumbled down the hill,
A sight so silly, it gave us a thrill.

A wise old owl perched in a tree,
Chided the fox, "Come dance with me!"
But the fox just rolled, quite out of luck,
Saying, "Who knew roots had such a knack for muck?"

Ants marched by with a tiny drum,
Leading a parade, oh what fun!
The fox joined in, quite proud of his strut,
Waving to squirrels who laughed at his butt!

As dusk crept in, the mischief grew,
Each critter joined the madness too.
In a world of humor wrapped in knits,
Every twist and turn just fits.

Legends in the Leaf Carpet

Amidst the leaves, a tale unfolds,
Of a mouse with dreams so bold.
He sought a crown made of acorns,
In a kingdom ruled by cheeky fawns.

They giggled and pranced, what a sight!
"Who needs a crown when you can bite?"
The mouse declared, "I'll still be king,
With these nutty treasures, I'll give you a zing!"

As night fell down and stars popped out,
A porcupine joined in, no doubt.
Spinning tales of bravery so grand,
With quills and all, he took a stand.

By morning light, their laughter soared,
The legends of leaves they all adored.
In the carpet beneath their feet,
Became the stories no one could beat.

The Harmony of Hoofbeats

In a glade where critters prance,
A horse and a turtle took a chance.
They danced in sync to a bouncy beat,
Each hoof and shell made the rhythm sweet.

Frogs joined in with a ribbit cheer,
As butterflies flitted, drawing near.
The horse said, "Faster, let's go wild!"
But the turtle just smiled, oh so mild.

A goat jumped in, quite out of time,
Adding a bounce, oh what a rhyme!
He tripped on a log, what a clumsy fall,
Yet laughed it off, standing proud and tall.

By dusk, the meadow rang with joy,
A symphony made by critters, oh boy!
In a harmony of hooves and glee,
Every thump and thud was pure jubilee.

Stories Among the Wildflowers

In a patch of bright daisies, a rabbit wore shades,
He danced like a breeze, through the sunlit glades.
A squirrel told jokes from a tall acorn tree,
While bees gathered laughter, sweet as can be.

The daisies all giggled, swaying in cheer,
A mushroom with puns joined in with good cheer.
They played hide and seek with a butterfly's flight,
And painted the meadow in colors of bright.

An owl in the corner was acting quite sly,
He whispered to flowers, oh my, oh my!
The ladybugs chuckled, rolled on their backs,
As the wildflowers schemed their next funny act.

As dusk turned the meadow to shades of deep blue,
The critters all gathered for one last "moo-hoo!"
They'd tell silly stories till stars took their cue,
In the world of wildflowers, giggles still brew.

Chronicles of the Enchanted Glade

In a glade that was hidden, a group of frogs leapt,
They'd croak out their secrets, while others just crept.
A fox with a mustache spun tales of great fright,
Of shadows that danced when the moon was just right.

A hedgehog in spectacles worked on his craft,
Drawing maps of the glade, with a giggle and laugh.
He said, "Follow me closely, I'll show you a prank,
Where the acorns grow tails, and the rivers turn crank!"

The owls were wise but loved a good jest,
They hooted with laughter, "We're up for a test!"
They staged a grand play, where they all wore a crown,
With berries as jewels, they twirled and fell down.

When night draped the glade in a silvery hue,
The creatures all gathered, with stories anew.
In the enchanted glade, laughter echoed so loud,
That even the moon smiled, wrapped in its shroud.

Murmurs of the Woodland Spirits

In the shade of the trees, where the whispers don't cease,
    Woodland spirits gather, their giggles increase.
    A sprite with a giggle-twist hid in the grass,
    Pulled pranks on the snails, who hadn't the sass.

    A wily old raccoon, with a hat made of leaves,
    Told tall tales of treasures that no one believes.
"Come find them!" he hollered, with a wink of his eye,
"Just follow the thickets where the humor flies high!"

While the fireflies twinkled, weaving light in a dance,
    The spirits made mischief, in a whimsical trance.
    A crow wore a tutu, flapping wings in delight,
        As the owls serenaded the magical night.

    In the woodland, a party of chuckles unfurled,
With laughter and mischief, a grand tale was twirled.
    For in this patch of wonder, the echoes of fun,
    Made the forest alive, in the warm setting sun.

Journeys Through the Mossy Maze

In a maze made of moss, with paths twisting all ways,
The critters embarked on peculiar displays.
A snail wore a backpack, with snacks made of cheese,
While a hedgehog mapped out, "Let's follow the breeze!"

They stumbled on mushrooms, all dressed for a ball,
Dancing with pixies, who invited them all.
A bear with a bowtie laughed loud at the sight,
Of a rabbit doing flips in the shimmering light.

The owl's hoot was the music, the melody sweet,
As they joined in a conga, in sync with their feet.
Hidden in shadows, the spirits would peep,
Chuckling at shenanigans that made them lose sleep.

When the maze finally ended, the sun dipped below,
The laughter echoed softly, as friendships would grow.
In journeys of joy, through the mossy embrace,
They found every turn brought a grin to each face.

Rambles in the Heart of the Thicket

In the woods where giggles grow,
Silly squirrels put on a show.
Twirling leaves in breezy dance,
A chubby fox joins without a chance.

Gigantic mushrooms wear hats so bright,
Bunnies hop with pure delight.
A wise old owl cracks a joke,
As laughter echoes 'neath the oak.

Underneath the twinkling glow,
Caterpillars put on a disco show.
Everyone joins in the fun-filled fray,
In the heart of the thicket, they all sway.

With playful pranks and endless cheer,
The creatures gather, having no fear.
They share their treats, a feast to see,
In their rambles, they're simply free.

Fables of the Flickering Shadows

In the twilight, shadows dance,
A hedgehog winks, he takes a chance.
Puppy dog tales fill the air,
While crickets chirp without a care.

A crow in shades, quite a sight,
Sings a tune with all his might.
An old raccoon spins a yarn,
Of treasure found, and the way to charm.

Silly shadows stretch and yawn,
While fireflies light the lawn.
Each whisper tickles the warm night air,
As stories weave without a care.

In the glow of the evening's bliss,
Every creature shares a wish.
With laughter, fables blend and play,
In flickering shades, they dance all day.

Secrets of the Sapphire Sky

The sky above, a brilliant blue,
Squirrels gossip, just a few.
They talk of nuts, so grand and nice,
While perched on branches, oh so precise.

A bird with swagger sings so loud,
His feathered friends, they gather proud.
With a wink and a nod, he shares his ways,
Of jumping clouds and sunny days.

The ants parade, all in a row,
Marching proudly, as they go.
Each tiny footstep a rhythmic beat,
Together they dance on little feet.

The sapphire sky holds secrets dear,
Of laughter ringing, far and near.
Under this dome, they frolic and fly,
Creating cheer as they touch the sky.

The Tapestry of Twigs and Tales

Amongst the twigs, a funny line,
A rabbit shares a glass of wine.
With twinkling eyes, he sips with glee,
While wondering if he'll dance with me.

A tapestry woven with giggles and cheer,
Each tale spun brings friends so near.
The trees sway, a rhythmic embrace,
As laughter fills this playful space.

Chubby chipmunks sing off-key,
While frogs jump in harmony.
Along the brook, they splash and play,
Together creating their own cabaret.

With whispers of fun and mischief's delight,
Each creature hops into the night.
This merry band beneath moonlight sails,
In the tapestry of twigs and tales.

Dreams in the Woodland's Embrace

In the woods where shadows play,
A squirrel juggles nuts all day.
The owl can't keep his eyes awake,
While rabbits dance for fun's own sake.

The tree stumps wear their hats so high,
A raccoon sings a song nearby.
With twigs for magic wands they tease,
As foxes prance among the leaves.

A hedgehog tells a tall, tall tale,
Of secret paths that all could fail.
The fireflies blink in delight,
As firewood cracks late into night.

And on the hill a party grows,
With mushrooms dancing in neat rows.
The woodland creatures laugh and cheer,
In dreams where nothing's far or near.

Myths of the Forgotten Glens

Beneath the boughs, a badger grins,
His stories swirl like dust on winds.
He spins of giants made of cheese,
And mermaids with a knack to sneeze.

One froggy prince claims he can sing,
But croaks just cause the birds to wing.
A mouse in boots declares the quest,
To find the socks of all the rest.

A hedgehog's crown, it tips and sways,
While rabbits plan their grand displays.
The whispers echo through the night,
As shadows dance in moon's soft light.

With every twist and goofy laugh,
The fables shape a joyful path.
In glens forgotten, tales unfold,
Of antics fierce and hearts so bold.

Sagas of the Old Oak

The old oak tree, he knows it all,
From acorn dreams to tree-top ball.
He chuckles deep in bark-clad glee,
While ants debate their next big spree.

With branches wide, he spreads the goss,
Of caterpillars crossed and lost.
A woodpecker taps a sneaky beat,
While squirrels bicker o'er a treat.

A dragonfly, with jeweled wings,
Claims magic in the song she sings.
While beetles march in grand parades,
Creating mischief in the glades.

And as the sun begins to set,
The laughter stays, it won't forget.
Old oak stands proud, with tales to share,
Of woodland laughs that fill the air.

Romances in the Fern Fronds

In fronds of green where whispers twine,
Two snails declare their love divine.
A peacock struts but trips in pride,
While ladybugs emerge and glide.

The toadstools host a dance so sweet,
With fireflies tapping tiny feet.
They twirl and spin beneath the moon,
While shadows play a cheeky tune.

A fox seeks love beneath the stars,
But stumbles into wayward jars.
While hedgehogs trade their spiky charms,
To win the heart of leafy arms.

The ferns, they sway with gentle grace,
As laughter blooms in every place.
Romantic mischief fills the night,
In woodland hearts, all feels just right.

Chronicles of the Underbrush

In the thicket, a squirrel chases his tail,
Dodging a beetle wearing a tiny mail.
A rabbit sneezes, causing a scene,
While a mouse in the corner sips on a bean.

Nearby, a hedgehog peers through the leaves,
Arguing with a crow that steals from the eaves.
"I don't share food, not even a crumb!"
But the crow just caws, thinking it fun.

A fox in a vest barges into the fray,
Dancing a jig as he shouts, "Hooray!"
The thorns and the bramble join in the jest,
Laughing with glee in their leafy fest.

All creatures gathered for laughter and cheer,
In the wild underbrush, not a single fear.
With antics so silly, it's hard to take pause,
In this lively banquet, no one's a lost cause.

Echoes in the Green Depths

In a glade, a frog tells a joke to a hare,
Who giggles so hard, he tumbles in air.
The fireflies wink, joining in to declare,
Life is a circus; we're all in the fair!

A turtle tries breakdancing, oh what a sight,
Spinning 'round slowly, with all of his might.
While a curious fox plays the drums on a log,
And the bushes respond with a rustle and fog.

An owl in spectacles drops by for a drink,
And offers his wisdom while we laugh and think.
"Life's just a hoot if you take it with glee!"
"But mind the raccoon who's stolen your brie!"

Under the canopy, joy swirls around,
With giggles and chuckles in every sound.
In the thick of the greens, where the fun never ends,
All creatures are welcome, from foes to old friends.

Shadows Among the Shrubs

A raccoon in shadows, sneaky and sly,
Tricked a small lizard, who thought he could fly.
"Just jump off this branch! It's easy, I swear!"
But lizard lands softly, with the utmost care.

A hedgehog complains of the tickles from grass,
While a beetle rolls by wearing sunglasses.
"I know it's sunny, but shade's where it's at!"
Echoes the parrot, perched high on a bat.

Each frond holds a story, each twig a good grin,
Where wisecracks and giggles just always begin.
The shadows are filled with the laughs of the night,
As creatures all gather, in pure delight.

Chortles and chuckles, they bubble and rise,
Under the shrubs, much to everyone's surprise.
With comedy blooming under moonlight so bright,
The thicket transforms into a stand-up night.

Fables of the Ferns

The ferns whisper secrets, all leafy and green,
Of a chubby old badger who loves to be seen.
He wears vibrant shorts and a sun hat so wide,
Strutting with flair on the forest's pride.

A mischievous raccoon pulls pranks from the mist,
While a turtle tries hiding, but can't resist.
The ferns giggle softly, their leaves all a-twirl,
As bugs dance around, giving summer a whirl.

In the shade of the fronds, a party unfolds,
With punch made of berries and laughter pure gold.
Each critter takes turns telling jokes of their day,
As the wise old owl hoots, "Let's all play!"

So gather, dear friends, in this whimsical glade,
Where the fables of ferns bring a joy parade.
With humor and kindness, the night stretches long,
In the heart of the thicket, we all sing along.

Enigmas of the Thorns

In a patch where roses meet,
A hedgehog dances on tiny feet.
Wearing a hat, quite out of place,
He moves with grace, all over the space.

A squirrel juggles acorns with flair,
But drops one right into my hair.
Laughter erupts from the nearby vines,
As wisdom grows on twisted pines.

The Stories Weave in the Briar

A spider spins tales of woe,
But giggles when the winds blow.
His web a stage for clumsy flies,
Who take a bow, then say their goodbyes.

In shadows bright, the rabbits hop,
Bouncing high, they never stop.
They make a game of hide and seek,
While climbing up a tall, thin peak.

Adventures Among the Wildflowers

Butterflies hold a festival grand,
With ladybugs forming a marching band.
They twirl and sway to a buzzing tune,
As daisies cheer beneath the moon.

A bumblebee lost in his flight,
Stops for nectar, what a sight!
He trips and tumbles, buzzing loud,
While wildflowers giggle, oh so proud.

Serpents and Spirits of the Dell

A snake in sunglasses sips his tea,
He chuckles, 'Life's easy for me!'
With a twirl, he gives a wink,
And makes the bushes pause to think.

The spirits play pranks by the brook,
With wild antics, like in a book.
They throw a splash, and laughter rolls,
As everyone joins in, to lift their souls.

Parables in the Patchwork Understory

Amidst the leaves, the rabbits plot,
A scheme so clever, yet they forgot.
The carrots lie low, just out of sight,
While the fox laughs, ready to bite.

Squirrels debate, the acorns to hoard,
While the owl snoozes, oh how they snored!
A nutty affair, a gathering spree,
With snacks falling down like it's free!

The hedgehog joins with a spiky grin,
He thinks he's the fastest, but where to begin?
While the tortoise chuckles, moves slow as a snail,
In this patchwork tale, they all seem to fail.

At dusk they all gather, a whimsical sight,
To share their mischief, day turned to night.
With a chuckle and cheer, under stars overhead,
In the patchwork understory, all worries are shed.

The Silent Watchers of the Woods

In quiet corners, whispers abound,
With critters conspiring without a sound.
The trees stand tall like judges unkind,
As the mischief unfolds, oh dear, never blind!

A squirrel plays dress-up, in leaves so bright,
While the birds roll their eyes, what a sight!
The raccoon is plotting a late-night feast,
With cookies and crumbs, he's surely the beast!

The owls are chuckling, their eyes all aglow,
Watching the mayhem, putting on a show.
The shadows grow longer, laughter does hum,
In the woods so alive, where silliness comes.

With each tiny sound, a story gets spun,
Of woodland trips under the moon and sun.
The silent watchers, ever so sly,
Record every giggle that flutters on by.

The Dance of Dewdrops and Dreams

Dewdrops twinkle, like stars on the grass,
As critters convene for the fun that won't pass.
The toads start croaking, a ribbiting beat,
While bunnies do cha-cha with rapid small feet!

The ladybugs waltz, in polka-dot lines,
While fireflies twinkle like bright little signs.
A misstep from mouse sends him spinning 'round,
And giggles erupt from the leaves on the ground.

Grasshoppers leap with a jubilant flair,
As the raccoons join in with their typical dare.
With a snicker and wiggle, they all twirl and sway,
In this dew-kissed dance where they frolic and play.

As moonlight sinks in, the dance starts to fade,
But laughter lingers, a sweet serenade.
With dreams taking flight, they swirl to their beds,
In the hush of the night, where joy never sheds.

Chronicles of the Wilted Blooms

In a garden once grand, where flowers would bloom,
Lived a pot of daisies with plenty of room.
But their friends, the weeds, had a different plan,
To throw a grand party, oh, yes, they began!

The roses complained, "We're wilting with shame!"
As the daisies danced wild, feeling no blame.
With the sun shining down, they twirled in delight,
While the thorns rolled their eyes, kept out of sight.

The snails were the bouncers, so slow and quite glum,
Taking their time, saying, "You'll need to come!"
While the bees brought the honey, the best of the sweets,
In this wild botanical bash, everyone eats!

As nightfall arrived, the petals grew tired,
But laughter resounded, their spirits inspired.
In chronicles written of blossoms and woes,
The wilted blooms laughed, as the garden still glows.

Legends of the Winding Path

In a forest where squirrels wear hats,
The raccoons debate where the cheese is at.
A turtle once claimed he could dance on a log,
But slipped and fell right onto a frog.

The fox tells a joke about a lost shoe,
While the owls hoot, 'That's nothing new!'
The trees stretch their branches, waving hello,
To the rabbits who prefer to hop slow.

Whispers echo of a bear who could sing,
He crooned out a tune, gave the squirrels bling.
Yet when he hit high notes, the honey did spill,
Now bees chase him down the hill with a thrill!

At the end of the path, there's a party, hooray!
Where critters play games till the break of day.
With laughter and snacks of the finest cuisine,
In the woods, we are part of this jovial scene.

Mysteries of the Leafy Labyrinth

In the maze where the hedges are wild and tall,
A raccoon in goggles claims he knows it all.
He spins silly tales of the paths that he roamed,
But got lost for an hour and just phoned home!

A rabbit once found a secretive door,
With a sign that read, 'Beware, gobbles galore!'
He peeked inside, took one bold bite,
But the pie was a trap—now he hops in fright!

The hedgehogs gossip about the strange map,
With arrows that point to the local mishap.
They giggle and nudge as they plan out a scheme,
To navigate life like a wild, wacky dream.

But in this lush maze, the secrets are clear,
It's laughter and friendship that bring us good cheer.
So let's roam together, through shadows and light,
And spin all our mysteries into sheer delight!

Song of the Forgotten Ferns

Once ferns threw a party but no one could tell,
For the crickets were singing, 'Oh do come and dwell!'
Yet the ferns just sat still, thinking, 'What a scene!'
While the mushrooms tapped feet, saying, 'We're keen!'

One fern, feeling bold, said, 'I'll show off my dance!'
And twirled in a way that enchanted a chance.
But slipped on some dew and fell with a plop,
Now the bros call him Ferny, the king of the flop!

They giggle and wiggle, all slimy and green,
With the ferns on the floor, creating a scene.
If you listen real close, you might hear a tune,
That the ferns sing at night by the light of the moon.

So join in the laughter, forget the old norms,
In the dance of the ferns, merriment warms.
Who knew plants could party, with roots in the air?
Let's sway until morning, without a single care!

Threads of the Twisted Vines

In a garden where vines loop and twine with delight,
A snail and a spider had a weaving fight.
They tangled their threads, what a colorful splash,
And soon called for help—'Oh, get us out fast!'

The bees buzz around, saying, 'What a great mess!'
While the ladybugs giggle, feeling quite blessed.
They joined in the fray, with their nimble little feet,
And soon formed a team, a peculiar fleet.

Now the vines weave stories, a tapestry bold,
With giggles and hiccups and laughter to hold.
Each twist tells a tale of the fun that we share,
In our wild, wiggly world, there's joy everywhere!

So let's dance with the vines, let our spirits unwind,
In a garden of giggles, where love is entwined.
With every small chuckle, let's cherish and cheer,
In the threads of the garden, we're happy right here!

Reveries in the Rustling Brush

In the undergrowth, a squirrel pranced,
Chasing shadows, he looked quite enhanced.
A rabbit slid by, in a coat of fine fur,
Claiming he'd found the best carrot blur.

A hedgehog with glasses, a book he did share,
Said, "Life's quite a page, don't you dare tear!"
The fox rolled his eyes, with laughter in tow,
Wishing for snacks and a nice place to grow.

A dance in the leaves, where the critters convene,
With a beat of the drums, from a hidden machine.
Each creature unique, with quirks of their own,
In a world of oddities they proudly have grown.

In the rustling brush where the giggles align,
Life's a grand story, and all creatures shine.
So join in the fun, let your worries release,
For a whimsical romp surely brings us peace.

Whimsy of the Wayward Beasts

A raccoon with a hat, oh what a sight,
Sipping on honey, feeling quite right.
The owls tossed confetti, and the mice spun in glee,
While the moon winked down, as if part of the spree.

A porcupine juggled his quills in a row,
While a cat on a skateboard put on quite the show.
The badger barked jokes, with a mischievous grin,
And a chorus of laughter erupted within.

A party in shadows, where the wild things play,
Every creature joined in, in their own funny way.
A goat told tall tales that defied every law,
Spinning yarns of adventures that left them in awe.

With promises of cookies and sweet berry pie,
The wayward beasts danced 'neath the starry sky.
Thus the night rolled on, in delightful surprise,
With joy in abundance, beneath twinkling skies.

Adventures in the Secret Arbor

In the secret arbor, where the critters convene,
Lies a gopher who dreams of vast lands green.
His burrows of treasure, oh what a find,
With shiny old buttons and gumdrops entwined.

The birds chirped stories of dragons and kings,
While a chipmunk exclaimed, "I'm the lord of all things!"

With tiny blue spectacles perched on his nose,
He claimed he could see how the wild magic grows.

An adventure unraveled, as they searched near the brook,
For a mythical creature, a rare storybook.
With giggles and squeals, they marched to the beat,
As laughter exploded in the soft grass below their feet.

In the heart of the arbor, where the oddballs could roam,
A world full of wonders, each patch felt like home.
So let's raise our cups made of dandelion foam,
To adventures unfolding in nature's grand dome!

Enigmas from the Gloomy Thicket

In the gloomy thicket, where whispers reside,
A bear with a riddle took pride as his guide.
"What walks on four legs then two, then three?"
Said the wise little sparrow, "Is it you or is me?"

An owl played detective in a trench coat so sleek,
Finding clues in the shadows, with a keen little squeak.
While a turtle, quite puzzled, calculated time,
Confounding the fox with his mathematical rhyme.

With comical clues intertwined in the fray,
The creatures all shouted, "Just join in the play!"
A riddle or two, they asked for delight,
And the fireflies twinkled, as day turned to night.

Yet amid all the laughter, a mystery remained,
Of who stole the pie that the hedgehog had claimed.
As they danced in the dusk, a conclusion they sought,
In the thicket of giggles, the answer was bought!

Legends held in the Lattice of Leaves

In a wooded dance, the squirrels conspire,
Crafting their myths, fueled by desire.
Acorns are gold, in their secret stash,
Somersaults lead to a nutty splash.

Frogs in the pond croak tales of old,
Boasting of leaps, so brave and bold.
The rabbits giggle, ears flapping wide,
In a patchwork tale, their antics collide.

Mice moonlight-sneak, with cheese in a sack,
Tripping on roots, then making their track.
The owls from above hoot wisdom with flair,
While knowing full well, they're just below air.

With twinkling eyes, the hedgehogs delight,
In their prickly armor, they take winged flight.
Legends are spun amidst branches and leaves,
Where laughter takes root and mirth never leaves.

Reverberations of the Sunbeam Path

Sunbeams tickle, the day comes alive,
The ants throw a party, where six-legged thrive.
With crumbs of delight, they dance in the light,
Their tiny confetti makes everything bright.

Bees buzz in joy, crafting honey with cheer,
While flowers giggle, 'We love when you're near!'
The butterflies flit, draped in color galore,
Stirring up mischief, while chasing the lore.

A grasshopper snaps, setting rhythms so sweet,
The beetles parade in a marching retreat.
Each sound ebbs and flows on the sunbeam's warm track,
As the forest joins in, there's no looking back.

Laughter echoes through branches so tall,
In this vibrant maze, all creatures stand small.
With echoes of mirth dancing under the sun,
On the path of the beams, every day is pure fun.

Tales of the Enigmatic Echoes

In shadows of mystery, whispers abound,
Where echoes of laughter spin round and round.
The fox tells a secret to a curious hare,
Who winks with a grin, then vanishes in air.

A raccoon with mischief defies every rule,
Rummaging treasures, but playing the fool.
With hats made of leaves, he struts in the night,
While critters around can't help but delight.

Pigeons gossip loudly of scandalous schemes,
They dream of adventures, or so it seems.
While beneath the old oak, a turtle takes bets,
On who'll be the fastest in quirky duets.

All wildlife confounds with their comical tales,
A menagerie spawned from their quirky travails.
In echoes of laughter, life blooms so thick,
For each twist and turn is a whimsical trick.

The Twilight's Gentle Tangle

As night softly blankets the world in a hush,
The critters emerge in a jovial rush.
Fireflies sparkle, drawing soft giggles,
With each twinkling glimmer, childhood wiggles.

The owls swap stories as shadows intertwine,
While rabbits discuss their best underground wine.
With a sprinkle of mischief, the hedgehogs unite,
To share tales of bravado from deep in the night.

Crickets compose symphonies, sweet and bizarre,
While a sleepy old toad measures coolness by far.
With his tiny top hat and antics profound,
He croons soft dirges as friends gather round.

In twilight's embrace, where laughter sets sail,
Each creature's a star in this humorous tale.
With tales of enchantment, the night never lags,
For in this fine tangle, joy happily brags.

Dreams in the Dappled Shade

Bunnies wear hats, they're quite the sight,
Sipping on tea by the soft moonlight.
Twirling in dresses made of leaves,
They dance in circles, just like thieves.

Squirrels play cards with a fox named Lou,
Bets of acorns, and cheese fondue.
A parrot squawks, 'You've lost again!'
While the deer laugh loud, saying, 'What a hen!'

In the shadows, a raccoon sneaks,
Stealing their snacks with occasional squeaks.
'Oh no, not again!' cries the fluttering owl,
As laughter erupts through trees that scowl.

Soon bedtime calls, their giggles subside,
With dreams of mischief, they snuggle and hide.
In the morning light, they'll rise once more,
For the antics and joy that they all adore.

Whirlwinds of Whimsy in the Wild

A hedgehog in boots struts down the lane,
While a frog plays the banjo, it's quite insane!
The bear juggles berries, oh what a show,
And the bees buzz along, humming a flow.

The raccoon wears glasses, reading a tome,
About a brave mouse who traveled far from home.
With cookies in tow, and a grin ear to ear,
They laugh at the tales spun from cold winter's beer.

A whirlwind of giggles sweeps through the grass,
As chipmunks in capes dash away in a flash.
'Ugh, slow down!' cries a turtle, in quite the plight,
While a butterfly flutters, lighting up the night.

But as darkness falls, the fun starts to wane,
The forest settles down after all the gain.
With dreams of their frolics by starlight they'll wait,
For the dawn to bring new stories, oh what a fate!

The Dwellers of the Thicket

In a thicket where giggles are found,
The critters all gather, hopping around.
A badger named Bert tells the funniest jokes,
While the owls roll their eyes at the antics of folks.

A snail takes a selfie, all glossy and bright,
With a backdrop of flowers, oh what a sight!
A hedgehog photobombs, with a cheer and a grin,
Claiming it's him who should surely win.

The mouse in the corner is baking a cake,
But with each little move, oh, what a mistake!
Flour clouds rise as he fumbles and spills,
While laughter erupts, it's a riot of thrills.

As twilight approaches, they gather as one,
Sharing their stories, all spun just for fun.
With a promise of mischief for each brand-new day,
In their thicket of wonder, they'll giggle and play.

Vignettes of the Verdant Maze

In the maze of green where the giggles abound,
A parade of critters strolls round and round.
The raccoon wears ribbons; the skunk has a bow,
As they strut through the paths, putting on quite the show.

A wise old tortoise sings songs of the past,
While a silly grasshopper hops out at last.
He trips on a twig, falls down with a bounce,
And the laughter erupts—a collective flounce!

Down by the brook, the frogs start a band,
Playing fine tunes with a very loose hand.
The otters, meanwhile, splash water around,
Creating a whirlpool, the fun knows no bound.

And as stars peek out over evening's embrace,
They share all their chuckles, a warm, cozy space.
With whispers of antics lingering on air,
In the glow of the night, there's more joy to share.

Lament of the Fast-Fading Sun

The sun slips low, a golden drop,
A squirrel beneath, says, "Don't stop!"
His acorn stash, a treasure grand,
Yet shadows sneak, as night takes stand.

He grumbles loud, with furrowed brow,
"Dear sun, just hang for one more hour!"
But clouds are thick, like soup on stew,
He pouts, then scampers—what else to do?

His friends all tease, a merry crowd,
"Come join us now, don't make us loud!"
He rolls his eyes, but joins the jest,
And laughs with friends, that's for the best!

The fading sun, it doesn't mind,
While thickets echo with laughter combined.
With giggles bright, they bid farewell,
To a day that slipped away like a spell.

Journey into the Tangled Realm

A hedgehog packs his tiny bag,
With dreams of snacks and a chance to brag.
He steps outside, the twigs do crack,
"What's that?" he jumps, then shrinks back.

A bushy tail twirls by his side,
A cheeky fox with mischief wide.
"Come on, dear friend, let's have a snack,
Or shall we dance? There's no turn back!"

They tiptoe past the grumpy owl,
Whose nap was loud, instead of prowl.
With giggles shared, they dodge his glare,
And chase moonbeams without a care.

In thickets deep, where secrets play,
Their laughter bounces, night turns to day.
For tangled paths lead far and wide,
With friends beside, it's quite a ride!

Beneath the Bark's Embrace

A wise old tree, with bark so gray,
Holds secrets tight for a game to play.
The ants march in, a tiny parade,
While rabbits sneak snacks in the shade.

"Why sit and fret, when fun awaits?"
The tree chuckles, as moonlight mates.
"Each critter here has tales to spin,
Of clumsy leaps and points to win!"

As beetles roll rocks for a race,
The fireflies glow, lighting the space.
With whispers soft from breezy night,
They dance in shadows, a joyful sight.

Beneath this bark, let giggles flow,
For every branch has a tale to show.
In nature's cradle, laughs take flight,
And dreams emerge in the twinkling light.

Melodies from the Rustling Grass

In fields of green where crickets croon,
A chorus bubbles 'neath the moon.
The grasshoppers jump, showcasing flair,
As beetles tap dance, without a care.

"Let's start a band!" a voice does sing,
The frogs join in, with a ribbeting ring.
The winds hum softly, like whispers bold,
As nature's symphony unfolds.

With notes that cheekily bounce and swirl,
The daisies sway, in a concert whirl.
A hedgehog claps, with great delight,
"More beats, more fun! Let's dance all night!"

So here they gather, friends in a trance,
With melodies rich, they prance and prance.
For laughter reigns where music plays,
In rustling grass, joy fills their days.

www.ingramcontent.com/pod-product-compliance
Lightning Source LLC
Chambersburg PA
CBHW051646160426
43209CB00004B/804